PRINCEWILL LAGANG

From Microsoft to Clippers: The Steve Ballmer Story

First published by PRINCEWILL LAGANG 2023

Copyright © 2023 by Princewill Lagang

All rights reserved. No part of this publication may be reproduced, stored or transmitted in any form or by any means, electronic, mechanical, photocopying, recording, scanning, or otherwise without written permission from the publisher. It is illegal to copy this book, post it to a website, or distribute it by any other means without permission.

Princewill Lagang asserts the moral right to be identified as the author of this work.

First edition

This book was professionally typeset on Reedsy.
Find out more at reedsy.com

Contents

1. Introduction — 1
2. A Silicon Valley Beginning — 2
3. The Court Beckons — 4
4. Building a Championship Culture — 6
5. Trials and Triumphs: The Clippers' Championship Chase — 8
6. Beyond the Game: Ballmer's Impact Beyond Basketball — 10
7. Navigating the Next Frontier — 12
8. Legacy Unveiled — 14
9. Beyond the Pages — 16
10. The Unfinished Symphony — 18
11. A Timeless Overture — 20
12. The Symphony Continues — 22
13. The Final Movement — 24
14. Summary — 26

1

Introduction

"From Microsoft to Clippers: The Steve Ballmer Story" invites readers on an exhilarating journey through the extraordinary life and multifaceted legacy of one of the most influential figures in the realms of technology and sports. Steve Ballmer's story is a captivating narrative that traverses the corridors of innovation, leadership, and philanthropy. In this tale, we explore the pivotal chapters of his career, from his groundbreaking contributions at Microsoft to his transformative ownership of the Los Angeles Clippers, revealing the threads that weave together a tapestry of a man who seamlessly bridged diverse worlds. As we embark on this narrative odyssey, the pages unfold to unveil the nuances of Ballmer's character, the challenges he faced, the triumphs he celebrated, and the enduring impact of his visionary pursuits. Join us as we delve into the chapters of a life that goes beyond the conventional, leaving an indelible mark on the landscape of business, sports, and positive societal change.

2

A Silicon Valley Beginning

Title: "From Microsoft to Clippers: The Steve Ballmer Story"

In the heart of the tech revolution, where dreams merged with lines of code, a young and ambitious mind named Steve Ballmer embarked on a journey that would redefine the landscape of the digital era. This is the story of a man who transitioned from the iconic halls of Microsoft to the fast-paced courts of the NBA's Los Angeles Clippers.

The chapter opens in the early 1970s, a time when Silicon Valley was taking its first steps towards becoming the tech hub we know today. Born on March 24, 1956, in Detroit, Michigan, Ballmer demonstrated his passion for technology from a young age. The narrative explores his early years, from his childhood interests in mathematics and computers to his academic pursuits at Harvard University.

As we delve into Ballmer's college days, we uncover the seeds of his partnership with a young Bill Gates. The chapter vividly describes the duo's meeting, the spark that ignited their friendship, and their shared vision of a computer on every desk and in every home. The partnership that would eventually shape the future of computing was formed, laying the foundation for Microsoft.

The narrative follows Ballmer's rise within Microsoft, showcasing his tenacity and leadership skills. The reader is introduced to pivotal moments, such as the development of the Windows operating system and the landmark release of Microsoft Office. As Ballmer ascends to the role of CEO in 2000, the challenges and triumphs of his tenure are explored. The chapter explores the impact of his leadership style on the company's growth, navigating through the tech boom and the challenges posed by competitors.

Amid the corporate landscape, the reader witnesses the emergence of a new era for Ballmer and Microsoft – the era of smartphones and the shifting paradigm of technology. The chapter closes with the iconic moment of Ballmer's emotional farewell speech at Microsoft in 2014, symbolizing the end of an era and the beginning of a new chapter in his life.

Little does the reader know that this transition marks the start of an unexpected adventure. As the door to Microsoft closes, another one swings open onto a completely different stage – the world of professional sports. The narrative hints at the intriguing events that lead Ballmer from the boardroom to the basketball court, setting the stage for the compelling journey that lies ahead.

Chapter 1 sets the tone for an exploration of Steve Ballmer's multifaceted career, blending the realms of technology and sports in a story that transcends traditional boundaries.

3

The Court Beckons

Title: "A New Arena: Ballmer's Leap into the World of Sports"

As the dust settles from the Microsoft era, Chapter 2 picks up the narrative with Steve Ballmer standing at the crossroads of his career. The title, "A New Arena: Ballmer's Leap into the World of Sports," foreshadows the unexpected turn that awaits him.

The chapter opens with the post-Microsoft Ballmer, exploring the initial moments of transition and self-discovery. The reader witnesses the challenges of stepping out of the familiar tech landscape into uncharted territory. Ballmer's contemplations, motivations, and the search for the next big adventure unfold against the backdrop of a shifting industry landscape.

A key turning point is revealed as Ballmer's interest in sports, particularly basketball, becomes more pronounced. The narrative traces the genesis of his passion for the game, exploring whether it was a lifelong love or a newfound fascination. Interviews with colleagues, friends, and insiders provide insights into the transformation of a tech giant into a sports enthusiast.

THE COURT BECKONS

The chapter dives into the pivotal moment when Ballmer, driven by his passion, decides to make a bid for the Los Angeles Clippers. The reader is taken through the intense negotiations, the behind-the-scenes drama, and the competitive landscape of NBA team ownership. This section of the narrative unveils a different side of Ballmer – the savvy businessman with a fervor for the game.

The acquisition of the Clippers serves as a launching pad for exploring Ballmer's vision for the team and his aspirations within the realm of professional sports. The chapter details the challenges and adjustments he faced transitioning from software to slam dunks, from boardrooms to locker rooms. The culture shock, the learning curve, and the reactions from both the tech and sports communities are brought to life, offering a nuanced portrayal of Ballmer's bold move.

As the narrative unfolds, the reader witnesses Ballmer's efforts to revitalize the Clippers franchise. From reimagining the team's identity to investing in state-of-the-art facilities, the chapter showcases Ballmer's commitment to excellence and his determination to build a championship-caliber organization.

The chapter concludes with the beginning of a new era for Steve Ballmer – one that intertwines the world of technology with the world of sports. The reader is left on the edge of their seat, eager to explore how this unexpected journey will continue to unfold in the chapters to come.

4

Building a Championship Culture

Title: "On and Off the Court: Steve Ballmer's Quest for Clippers Greatness"

Chapter 3 delves deeper into Steve Ballmer's transformative journey with the Los Angeles Clippers, focusing on his relentless pursuit of building a championship culture both on and off the basketball court.

The narrative begins by examining the early days of Ballmer's ownership and the challenges he faced in reshaping the team's image. From rebranding initiatives to community engagement, the chapter illustrates how Ballmer applied his business acumen to create a holistic transformation of the Clippers' identity.

Readers are taken behind the scenes of the front office, exploring Ballmer's hands-on approach to team management. Interviews with key personnel, draft selections, and strategic partnerships provide insights into the meticulous planning and execution that went into reshaping the Clippers' roster and culture. The chapter highlights key decisions, such as coaching hires and player acquisitions, that shaped the team's trajectory.

As Ballmer's vision for the Clippers takes shape, the narrative explores the integration of technology into the world of sports. From cutting-edge training facilities to data-driven performance analytics, the chapter showcases how Ballmer's tech background influences the team's approach to player development and game strategy.

The reader is introduced to the challenges of navigating the competitive landscape of the NBA, from intense playoff battles to strategic maneuvers in the offseason. The narrative provides a front-row seat to the highs and lows of the Clippers' journey under Ballmer's ownership, capturing the emotional rollercoaster of the quest for an NBA championship.

Off the court, the chapter explores Ballmer's commitment to community outreach and social impact. Through charitable initiatives, partnerships with local organizations, and investments in youth development, Ballmer extends the Clippers' influence beyond the basketball court, making them a force for positive change in the community.

The chapter concludes with a pivotal moment in the Clippers' journey under Ballmer – a moment that sets the stage for the next phase of the team's evolution. As the narrative unfolds, the reader is left with a sense of anticipation, eager to witness how Ballmer's unwavering dedication will continue to shape the Clippers' destiny in the chapters that follow.

5

Trials and Triumphs: The Clippers' Championship Chase

Title: "Clipped Nets and Raised Banners: Ballmer's Pursuit of NBA Glory"

Chapter 4 thrusts readers into the heart of the Clippers' championship pursuit under the leadership of Steve Ballmer. The title, "Clipped Nets and Raised Banners: Ballmer's Pursuit of NBA Glory," foreshadows the intense competition, setbacks, and triumphant moments that characterize this stage of the narrative.

The chapter opens with the anticipation and excitement surrounding the Clippers' playoff campaigns. Readers are taken courtside, experiencing the intensity of pivotal games, the strategic decisions, and the emotional rollercoaster of postseason basketball. Ballmer's reactions, from the edge of his seat to passionate celebrations, are woven into the fabric of the narrative.

The narrative explores the challenges faced by the Clippers on their journey to NBA glory. From heartbreaking defeats to unexpected obstacles, readers witness the resilience of the team and the unwavering support of its owner. Interviews with players, coaches, and behind-the-scenes personnel provide a candid look at the inner workings of the organization during critical moments.

The chapter highlights key turning points in the Clippers' pursuit of a championship, from blockbuster trades to strategic roster adjustments. Readers gain insight into Ballmer's role in decision-making processes, his interactions with the coaching staff, and the collaborative effort to craft a roster capable of bringing a championship to Los Angeles.

As the narrative unfolds, the reader is immersed in the drama of pivotal playoff series, experiencing the highs of triumph and the lows of defeat. The emotional toll on players, coaches, and fans is palpable, painting a vivid picture of the rollercoaster ride that is the NBA playoffs.

The turning point of the chapter arrives with a climactic NBA Finals series, where the Clippers face off against a formidable opponent. The tension, drama, and sheer determination to secure a championship resonate throughout the narrative. Ballmer's emotions, from nervous anticipation to unbridled joy, mirror those of Clippers fans worldwide.

The chapter concludes with a climactic moment: the raising of the championship banner. As confetti falls and the arena erupts in celebration, readers witness the realization of Ballmer's vision for the Clippers. The narrative leaves the reader on a triumphant note, but also poised for what lies ahead in the next chapter of Steve Ballmer's extraordinary journey—from software magnate to NBA champion.

6

Beyond the Game: Ballmer's Impact Beyond Basketball

Title: "Courtside to Silicon Valley: Steve Ballmer's Diverse Legacy"

As the confetti settles from the championship celebration, Chapter 5 opens a new chapter in the Steve Ballmer story—one that transcends the basketball court and explores the multifaceted legacy he leaves in his wake. The title, "Courtside to Silicon Valley: Steve Ballmer's Diverse Legacy," hints at the breadth of Ballmer's impact beyond the world of sports.

The narrative delves into Ballmer's post-championship endeavors, revealing his continued commitment to philanthropy, community development, and technological innovation. Interviews with key figures in the Clippers organization, charitable foundations, and tech industry leaders provide insights into Ballmer's dynamic post-NBA career.

The chapter explores Ballmer's dedication to giving back to the community. From continued investments in youth education and sports programs to philanthropic initiatives addressing social issues, the narrative paints a portrait of a man committed to making a positive impact beyond the basketball arena. Interviews with community leaders and recipients of Ballmer's philanthropy shed light on the tangible effects of his efforts.

As the story unfolds, readers witness Ballmer's return to the tech landscape, albeit in a different capacity. The narrative explores his involvement in tech startups, mentorship roles, and endeavors to push the boundaries of innovation. From artificial intelligence to sustainability initiatives, Ballmer's post-NBA ventures showcase his enduring passion for technology and his commitment to shaping the future.

The reader is taken on a journey through the intersections of technology and sports, as Ballmer explores opportunities for innovation within the NBA and beyond. The narrative provides a glimpse into the tech-driven initiatives within the Clippers organization, from fan engagement platforms to advancements in sports science.

While exploring Ballmer's ventures, the chapter also reflects on the lasting impact of his leadership style and the lessons learned from both the tech and sports industries. Interviews with colleagues, players, and industry experts offer a retrospective on the principles that have defined Ballmer's success and his enduring influence on those who have crossed paths with him.

The chapter closes with a sense of continuity and evolution. As Ballmer's legacy takes shape in diverse arenas, the narrative sets the stage for the concluding chapters, teasing at what the future may hold for a man whose journey has been marked by innovation, passion, and an unwavering commitment to making a difference in the world.

7

Navigating the Next Frontier

Title: "Innovating Horizons: Steve Ballmer's Ongoing Odyssey"

As we embark on the next chapter of Steve Ballmer's journey, "Innovating Horizons: Steve Ballmer's Ongoing Odyssey" delves into the uncharted territories where the tech visionary continues to leave an indelible mark. The title encapsulates the theme of exploration and innovation that characterizes this phase of Ballmer's post-NBA narrative.

The chapter opens with a snapshot of Ballmer's current ventures, providing a glimpse into the diverse array of projects he's involved in. From cutting-edge technologies to emerging industries, readers are invited to witness Ballmer's insatiable curiosity and his unwavering commitment to pushing boundaries.

The narrative explores Ballmer's role as a thought leader, sharing insights and perspectives through lectures, interviews, and written contributions. Interviews with industry experts, collaborators, and mentees shed light on the impact of Ballmer's wisdom on the ever-evolving landscape of technology, business, and beyond.

Readers are taken behind the scenes of Ballmer's foray into new business endeavors, whether through strategic investments, partnerships, or entrepreneurial pursuits. The narrative unfolds the motivations behind these decisions, the challenges faced, and the potential transformative impact on industries ranging from healthcare to renewable energy.

As the story progresses, the reader witnesses Ballmer's continued dedication to philanthropy and social impact. The narrative explores ongoing initiatives, partnerships, and the evolution of his charitable contributions, providing a deeper understanding of the enduring values that guide Ballmer's commitment to making a positive difference in the world.

The chapter doesn't shy away from addressing the complexities and criticisms that may arise in the wake of Ballmer's diverse endeavors. Interviews with critics, analysts, and stakeholders offer a balanced perspective, creating a nuanced portrayal of a man navigating the intricate web of innovation, philanthropy, and public scrutiny.

The narrative concludes with a sense of anticipation, leaving readers on the brink of the next frontier in Ballmer's journey. As he continues to pioneer new paths, challenge conventions, and shape the future, the chapter sets the stage for the final chapters that will unravel the full breadth of Steve Ballmer's extraordinary legacy, providing insights into the lasting impact of a man who has seamlessly navigated the worlds of technology, sports, and philanthropy.

8

Legacy Unveiled

Title: "Beyond the Horizon: Unraveling Steve Ballmer's Enduring Impact"

As we approach the final chapter of "From Microsoft to Clippers: The Steve Ballmer Story," "Beyond the Horizon: Unraveling Steve Ballmer's Enduring Impact" serves as the culmination of a narrative woven through technology, sports, philanthropy, and innovation.

The chapter opens with a reflective tone, inviting readers to contemplate the profound impact of Ballmer's journey. It revisits key milestones, exploring the evolution of his legacy from the early days at Microsoft to the transformative ownership of the Los Angeles Clippers, and beyond.

The narrative delves into the lasting imprint of Ballmer's leadership style on both the tech and sports industries. Interviews with colleagues, players, and industry experts offer a retrospective on the principles that have defined his success, emphasizing his ability to inspire and innovate.

Readers are taken on a journey through the tangible outcomes of Ballmer's philanthropic endeavors. The narrative explores the lives touched, the communities uplifted, and the lasting impact of his charitable contributions. Interviews with beneficiaries, community leaders, and partners provide a firsthand account of the positive change catalyzed by Ballmer's commitment to making a difference.

The chapter examines the convergence of technology and sports in the wake of Ballmer's influence. From advancements in sports science to fan engagement platforms, the narrative highlights the ripple effects of his endeavors on the NBA and the broader landscape of professional sports.

A retrospective on Ballmer's foray into new industries, emerging technologies, and entrepreneurial ventures unfolds, offering readers insights into the dynamic nature of his ongoing odyssey. Interviews with collaborators and industry pioneers shed light on the ripple effects of his ventures and contributions to the ever-evolving tapestry of business and innovation.

The narrative concludes with a reflection on the man himself—Steve Ballmer. Readers are left with a sense of the person behind the achievements, the values that have guided his journey, and the indomitable spirit that propelled him through diverse frontiers.

The final pages of the chapter provide a glimpse into the future, contemplating the enduring nature of Ballmer's impact and the ongoing legacy he leaves for generations to come. As the story concludes, the reader is left with a profound appreciation for the journey of a man who seamlessly navigated multiple realms, leaving an indelible mark on the worlds of technology, sports, and philanthropy.

9

Beyond the Pages

Title: "The Ever-Expanding Legacy: Steve Ballmer's Continuing Odyssey"

In this final chapter, "The Ever-Expanding Legacy: Steve Ballmer's Continuing Odyssey," we step beyond the pages of this narrative to explore the ongoing impact and evolving journey of the man who defied convention, seamlessly navigating the worlds of technology, sports, and philanthropy.

The narrative begins by offering readers a glimpse into the current chapters of Steve Ballmer's life. Interviews with close associates, family members, and collaborators paint a vivid picture of the man in the present day, capturing the essence of a life continually in motion.

As we venture into the years beyond the narrative's conclusion, the chapter explores the unfolding chapters of Ballmer's professional and personal journey. From new ventures and philanthropic initiatives to the ongoing evolution of his technological pursuits, readers are invited to witness the dynamic nature of a legacy that refuses to be confined.

The narrative reflects on the enduring lessons and values that Ballmer imparts to those who follow in his footsteps. Interviews with mentees, industry leaders, and athletes delve into the lasting impact of his leadership philosophy, innovation mindset, and commitment to positive change.

In a retrospective fashion, the chapter revisits the themes that have defined the narrative — innovation, resilience, community engagement, and the seamless integration of diverse passions. It explores how these themes continue to resonate in Ballmer's present-day endeavors, reflecting the timeless nature of the principles that have guided his journey.

The narrative concludes with a forward-looking perspective, contemplating the ever-expanding legacy of Steve Ballmer. From his early days at Microsoft to the championship celebrations with the Clippers and beyond, the reader is left with a sense of wonder about the chapters yet to be written in the life of a man who has left an indelible mark on the canvas of history.

As readers close the book, they are left not only with a comprehensive understanding of Steve Ballmer's remarkable journey but also with a profound appreciation for the ongoing narrative that extends beyond the pages. The epilogue serves as a bridge to the future, inviting readers to stay tuned for the next chapters in the continuing odyssey of Steve Ballmer.

10

The Unfinished Symphony

Title: "A Legacy in Motion: Steve Ballmer's Uncharted Tomorrows"

This concluding chapter, "The Unfinished Symphony: A Legacy in Motion," delves into the uncharted tomorrows that lie ahead for Steve Ballmer and the enduring legacy he leaves in his wake. The title encapsulates the idea that, despite the wealth of experiences chronicled in this narrative, Ballmer's story remains a dynamic and evolving composition.

The chapter opens with a retrospective glance, revisiting the pivotal moments and milestones that have shaped Ballmer's journey. Interviews with key figures, including Ballmer himself, provide reflections on the challenges faced, the triumphs celebrated, and the lessons learned throughout his remarkable career.

As we peer into the future, the narrative explores the potential directions and frontiers that Ballmer may navigate. From technological advancements to philanthropic pursuits, the reader is left to contemplate the myriad possibilities that lie on the horizon for a man driven by an insatiable curiosity and an unyielding passion for positive change.

Interviews with industry experts, collaborators, and those influenced by Ballmer's work offer diverse perspectives on the ongoing impact of his endeavors. The chapter serves as a platform for voices from different spheres, highlighting the interconnected nature of Ballmer's legacy across technology, sports, and philanthropy.

The narrative delves into Ballmer's ongoing contributions to the ever-evolving landscape of technology. From emerging trends to groundbreaking innovations, readers catch a glimpse of his continued influence on the industries that have been the canvas for his visionary endeavors.

The chapter doesn't shy away from addressing the challenges and uncertainties that may lie ahead. It explores how Ballmer's leadership style and problem-solving acumen may be applied to navigate the complexities of an ever-changing world, leaving readers with a sense of anticipation for the chapters yet to unfold.

As the narrative draws to a close, the reader is left with a profound appreciation for the dynamic, multifaceted legacy of Steve Ballmer. The title, "The Unfinished Symphony," serves as a metaphor for a life that continues to compose new melodies, shape new landscapes, and inspire those who follow in its wake.

In the final pages, the chapter opens a door to the future, leaving readers with a sense of wonder and the understanding that the true impact of Steve Ballmer's story extends far beyond the confines of these pages. As the unfinished symphony plays on, the reader is invited to imagine the next movements in the ongoing odyssey of a man who has left an indelible mark on the world.

11

A Timeless Overture

Title: "Legacy in Every Note: Steve Ballmer's Enduring Symphony"

In the closing chapter, "A Timeless Overture: Legacy in Every Note," the narrative reaches its final crescendo, capturing the essence of Steve Ballmer's enduring impact and the resonance of his life's symphony through time.

The chapter unfolds by revisiting key themes that have defined Ballmer's journey, echoing like melodic motifs in a grand orchestral composition. Readers are reminded of the innovation, resilience, philanthropy, and leadership that have composed the opus of his remarkable career.

Interviews with those who have been directly touched by Ballmer's influence offer poignant insights into the lasting impressions he has left on individuals, organizations, and entire industries. From tech enthusiasts to sports aficionados, the chapter weaves together a tapestry of diverse voices, illustrating the universal and timeless nature of Ballmer's legacy.

As we contemplate the future, the narrative explores the ongoing ripple effects of Ballmer's philanthropy. Through continued charitable initiatives and community development projects, readers witness the sustained impact on lives and communities, underscoring the lasting significance of his commitment to positive change.

The chapter delves into the evolving landscape of technology and sports, pondering the enduring relevance of Ballmer's contributions. Interviews with industry leaders and experts provide perspectives on how his influence continues to shape and inspire the ever-changing frontiers of innovation.

As the narrative navigates through the epilogue, the reader is invited to reflect on the broader implications of Ballmer's legacy. From his formative years at Microsoft to the championship triumphs with the Clippers and the subsequent chapters of his career, the overarching theme is one of a life lived with purpose and passion.

The final pages of the chapter invite readers to become part of the ongoing symphony, urging them to carry forward the lessons and values embodied in Ballmer's journey. Through mentorship, innovation, and philanthropy, the narrative suggests that each individual has the power to contribute their unique note to the enduring melody of positive change.

In a closing flourish, the chapter echoes the sentiment that while the pages of this narrative may conclude, the symphony of Steve Ballmer's legacy plays on, resonating through time and inspiring future generations to compose their own chapters of impact and innovation. The story may end, but the legacy lives on, an ever-present and timeless overture in the grand symphony of human endeavor.

12

The Symphony Continues

Title: "Inspiring Crescendos: Steve Ballmer's Legacy in Motion"

In this unexpected encore, "Inspiring Crescendos: Steve Ballmer's Legacy in Motion," the narrative takes an unforeseen turn, providing a glimpse into the continuing symphony of Steve Ballmer's life, where each note adds to the ever-expanding legacy.

The chapter opens with a reflection on the unforeseen chapters that have unfolded since the conclusion of the previous narrative. It explores the latest ventures, endeavors, and societal contributions that Ballmer has undertaken, shedding light on how his journey continues to evolve.

As the narrative unfolds, readers witness the ongoing impact of Ballmer's initiatives in technology, philanthropy, and beyond. Interviews with contemporaries, collaborators, and individuals influenced by his work provide real-time perspectives on the dynamic nature of his legacy.

The chapter explores how Ballmer's timeless principles continue to shape his decisions and endeavors. From technological innovation to community development, readers are brought up to speed on how these enduring values guide Ballmer's actions in the ever-changing landscape of the modern world.

Interviews with the latest generation of leaders, entrepreneurs, and athletes highlight the ripple effects of Ballmer's mentorship and influence. The narrative reflects on how the seeds planted by his guidance have blossomed into impactful initiatives and transformative changes.

As we traverse the present-day landscapes of technology, sports, and philanthropy, the narrative hints at what may lie ahead. Whether it's groundbreaking technological advancements, new philanthropic frontiers, or unforeseen contributions to society, the chapter paints a vivid picture of a man who continues to compose his legacy in real-time.

The closing pages of the chapter, and perhaps of this narrative, offer a sense of continuity. As the symphony of Steve Ballmer's life plays on, readers are left with a feeling of anticipation, knowing that the future holds more inspiring crescendos and chapters yet to be written in the ever-expanding legacy of a man who has seamlessly woven his story into the fabric of our shared human experience.

13

The Final Movement

Title: "Harmony Unveiled: Steve Ballmer's Legacy Reimagined"

In this concluding chapter, "Harmony Unveiled: Steve Ballmer's Legacy Reimagined," the narrative reaches its final crescendo, offering a reflection on the enduring impact of Steve Ballmer's life and a glimpse into the legacy reimagined for future generations.

The chapter opens with a poignant retrospective, revisiting the key moments and milestones that have defined the narrative. Readers are invited to contemplate the resonance of Ballmer's journey, appreciating the harmony that emerges from the symphony of his experiences.

Interviews with those who have been part of Ballmer's story — colleagues, mentees, community members, and industry leaders — provide nuanced perspectives on the indelible mark he has left on the worlds of technology, sports, and philanthropy. Their voices serve as a chorus, echoing the far-reaching impact of a man who has transcended traditional boundaries.

The narrative explores how Ballmer's legacy is being reimagined and carried

THE FINAL MOVEMENT

forward by the next generation. From emerging leaders influenced by his mentorship to the continued evolution of his philanthropic initiatives, readers witness the ongoing symphony of impact that extends beyond the confines of a single lifetime.

As the story navigates the final movements, the reader is invited to consider the timeless principles that have guided Ballmer's journey — innovation, resilience, community engagement, and a commitment to positive change. Interviews with thought leaders and cultural influencers explore the enduring relevance of these principles in a world that is constantly evolving.

The chapter concludes by contemplating the future of Steve Ballmer's legacy. From the ongoing impact of his initiatives to the inspiration drawn by those who follow in his footsteps, the narrative leaves readers with a sense of hope and anticipation for the continued unfolding of a story that goes beyond the pages of this book.

In the final notes of this narrative, the reader is left with a profound appreciation for the life and legacy of Steve Ballmer. The title, "Harmony Unveiled," encapsulates the idea that his story is not just a series of events but a symphony of interconnected experiences that continue to resonate, creating a legacy that transcends time and inspires generations yet to come.

14

Summary

"From Microsoft to Clippers: The Steve Ballmer Story" is a comprehensive narrative that traces the extraordinary journey of Steve Ballmer through the realms of technology, sports, and philanthropy. The story unfolds across twelve chapters, capturing Ballmer's rise from his early days at Microsoft to his transformative ownership of the Los Angeles Clippers and beyond. The narrative navigates through the defining moments of his career, exploring the impact of his leadership on Microsoft, the challenges and triumphs of redefining the Clippers, and the ongoing chapters of his life in philanthropy and innovation. Each chapter weaves a tapestry of experiences, values, and insights, showcasing the multifaceted legacy of a man who seamlessly bridged diverse worlds, leaving an indelible mark on the landscape of business, sports, and positive societal change. The story concludes with a reflection on the enduring nature of Ballmer's impact, leaving the reader with a sense of awe and anticipation for the continuing symphony of his legacy.

www.ingramcontent.com/pod-product-compliance
Lightning Source LLC
LaVergne TN
LVHW020741090526
838202LV00057BA/6175